BOOK 1 • E♭ Alto Saxophone          COMP...          IOD

# BEST IN CLASS

Dear Student,

Welcome to BEST IN CLASS!

Music is an important part of our daily lives. The study of music helps us gain an appreciation for beauty and a feeling of sensitivity. It also provides an avenue for creativity and recognition, as well as a demand for self-discipline. All of these are important in our world today.

Playing a musical instrument can also give you years of enjoyment. To play your instrument well, careful practice is essential. You will find a chart below to help you keep track of your practice time. Always strive to do your best.

Best wishes in reaching your musical goals!

Bruce Pearson

## PRACTICE RECORD CHART

| WEEK | DAY 1 | DAY 2 | DAY 3 | DAY 4 | DAY 5 | DAY 6 | DAY 7 | TOTAL TIME | PARENT'S INITIALS | WEEKLY GRADE |
|---|---|---|---|---|---|---|---|---|---|---|
| 1 | | | | | | | | | | |
| 2 | | | | | | | | | | |
| 3 | | | | | | | | | | |
| 4 | | | | | | | | | | |
| 5 | | | | | | | | | | |
| 6 | | | | | | | | | | |
| 7 | | | | | | | | | | |
| 8 | | | | | | | | | | |
| 9 | | | | | | | | | | |
| 10 | | | | | | | | | | |
| 11 | | | | | | | | | | |
| 12 | | | | | | | | | | |
| 13 | | | | | | | | | | |
| 14 | | | | | | | | | | |
| 15 | | | | | | | | | | |
| 16 | | | | | | | | | | |
| 17 | | | | | | | | | | |
| 18 | | | | | | | | | | |

| WEEK | DAY 1 | DAY 2 | DAY 3 | DAY 4 | DAY 5 | DAY 6 | DAY 7 | TOTAL TIME | PARENT'S INITIALS | WEEKLY GRADE |
|---|---|---|---|---|---|---|---|---|---|---|
| 19 | | | | | | | | | | |
| 20 | | | | | | | | | | |
| 21 | | | | | | | | | | |
| 22 | | | | | | | | | | |
| 23 | | | | | | | | | | |
| 24 | | | | | | | | | | |
| 25 | | | | | | | | | | |
| 26 | | | | | | | | | | |
| 27 | | | | | | | | | | |
| 28 | | | | | | | | | | |
| 29 | | | | | | | | | | |
| 30 | | | | | | | | | | |
| 31 | | | | | | | | | | |
| 32 | | | | | | | | | | |
| 33 | | | | | | | | | | |
| 34 | | | | | | | | | | |
| 35 | | | | | | | | | | |
| 36 | | | | | | | | | | |

© 1982 Neil A. Kjos Music Company, 4380 Jutland Drive, San Diego, California, 92117.
All Rights Reserved     International Copyright Secured     Printed in U.S.A.

BN  0-8497-5839-4          W3XE

# BEFORE YOU START...

## ASSEMBLING YOUR INSTRUMENT
- Remove the reed from its case and put it in your mouth to soak.
- Put the neck strap around your neck.
- Lubricate the **cork** on the **neck** with cork grease <u>as needed.</u>
- Remove your instrument from the case, hook it to the neck strap, and remove the end plug.
- Place the neck into the top of the instrument. Be careful not to bend the **octave key** or the **octave key lever.**
- Tighten the **neck screw.**
- With the weight of the saxophone on the neck strap and your knee, hold the neck with your LEFT hand. <u>Gently</u> twist on the **mouthpiece** so that approximately half of the cork is covered.
- Align the flat side of the mouthpiece with the octave key.

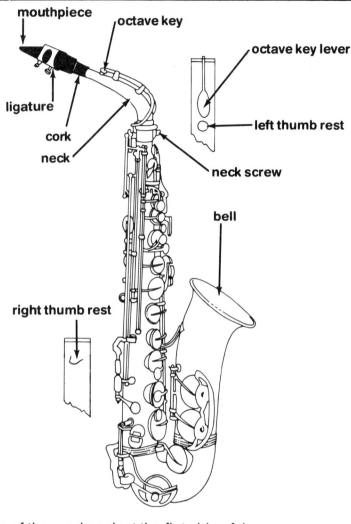

## PLACING THE REED ON THE MOUTHPIECE
- While resting the saxophone on your knee, place the **ligature** on the mouthpiece. The traditional ligature should be positioned so that the screws are on the flat side of the mouthpiece. Ask your director to check the positioning of the ligature.
- <u>Always protect the reed.</u>
- Push up the ligature with the thumb and first finger of one hand and slide the reed behind the ligature with the other hand. Keep the flat side of the reed against the flat side of the mouthpiece.
- Center the reed on the mouthpiece and position it so that only a hairline of black mouthpiece can be seen above the reed.
- Hold the reed in place with one hand, slide the ligature down, and <u>gently</u> tighten the ligature screws.

## HOLDING YOUR INSTRUMENT
- Place your RIGHT thumb under the **right thumb rest** at a point between the end of your thumb and first knuckle.
- Place your LEFT thumb diagonally on the **left thumb rest** so that it can easily operate the octave key lever.
- Place the fleshy part of your fingertips on the keys. Your fingers should curve naturally.
- Ask your director to check your hand positions.

# GETTING A GOOD TONE...

## POSITIONING YOUR INSTRUMENT
- Position your saxophone on the side of your RIGHT leg. The bottom of your saxophone should point toward the back leg of your chair.
- Adjust the neck strap so that the tip of your mouthpiece touches the center of your lower lip.
- Adjust your mouthpiece so that your head is held erect and straight, not at an angle.
- Ask your director to check the positioning of your saxophone.

## FORMING THE EMBOUCHURE
- Open your mouth so that your teeth are ⅜ inch apart.
- Cover your bottom teeth by slightly rolling your lower lip over your teeth.
- Hold your chin in a flat or pointed position. Many directors find that whistling creates this position.
- Place the mouthpiece in your mouth at the point where the reed separates from the mouthpiece. Ask your director to show you this spot. Reminder . . . be sure your bottom lip is covering your bottom teeth. Your top teeth will rest directly on the mouthpiece.
- Close your mouth muscles equally around the mouthpiece in a "drawstring" fashion. Firm up the corners of your mouth, keeping your chin pointed. Your teeth should remain slightly apart.
- Ask your director to check your embouchure.
- Check your embouchure regularly in front of a mirror.

## SITTING POSITION
- Sit on the edge of your chair, spine straight, shoulders back, and both feet flat on the floor.

## WIND SPEED
- Take a full breath by inhaling through the corners of your mouth.
- Be sure NOT to raise your shoulders while inhaling.
- GOOD WIND SPEED IS ESSENTIAL TO:
  1) Good tone quality
  2) Endurance
  3) Intonation
  4) Good tonguing

## STARTING EXERCISES
- "Air Game"
  1) Gently blow a steady stream of air through the mouthpiece WITHOUT MAKING A SOUND.
  2) Hear only the AIR going through the mouthpiece.
  3) Squeaking is a sign that either you are clamping your teeth too tightly or your reed is not adjusted properly.
  4) Use the "Air Game" occasionally to make sure your embouchure is not too tight.
- "One Tone Tooter"
  1) Speed the air up fast enough to produce a tone on your mouthpiece. (This should sound the pitch "A, one ledger line above the staff." )
  2) Your wind speed must make the reed vibrate. Do NOT clamp your teeth together.
  3) If the pitch is too high, your embouchure is too tight or your wind speed is too fast.
  4) If the pitch is too low, your embouchure is too loose or your wind speed is too slow.
- "Monotone March"
  1) Play a tone on your mouthpiece for 4 beats, then rest for 4 beats. Repeat this 4 times, keeping in mind all the points learned above.

# CARING FOR YOUR INSTRUMENT . . .

- Before putting your saxophone back in its case, do the following:
  1) Remove the reed. Wipe off the excess moisture with your fingers.
  2) Place the reed in its case so that it will dry thoroughly.
  3) Remove the mouthpiece and wipe out the inside with a soft clean cloth.
  4) Remove the neck and shake the moisture out of each end.
  5) Place the soft end of the neck cleaner into the large end of the neck. Draw it back and forth until the neck is dry.
  6) Drop the weight of the swab into the bell and out the other end. Pull the swab through the body several times.
  7) Wipe the connecting joint clean with the cloth.
  8) Wipe off the outside of your saxophone with the cloth.
- NEVER USE METAL POLISH ON YOUR SAXOPHONE.

# GETTING A HEAD START...

## THE BASICS

| KEYS | STAFF | TREBLE CLEF |
|---|---|---|
| o = key open <br> ● = key pressed down | ledger line | lines / spaces |

## THE "NATURAL" WAY TO START

### SITTING

Be sure you are sitting on the edge of your chair, spine straight, shoulders back, both feet flat on the floor.

**A. THE 1ST NOTE**

**B. THE 2ND NOTE**

**C. TWO'S COMPANY**

**D. A LITTLE EXTRA PRACTICE**

**E. THE 3RD NOTE**

**F. THREE TO GET READY**

**G. THREE STEPS**

**H. COMING BACK HOME**

**I. THE 4TH NOTE**

NEW NOTE

# for alto saxophones only

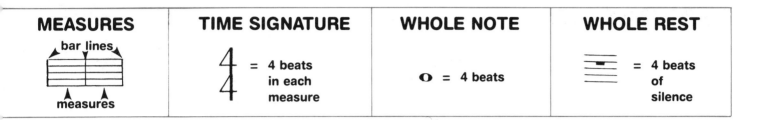

| MEASURES | TIME SIGNATURE | WHOLE NOTE | WHOLE REST |
|---|---|---|---|
| bar lines / measures | 4/4 = 4 beats in each measure | 𝅝 = 4 beats | ▬ = 4 beats of silence |

| HOLDING YOUR INSTRUMENT | PLAYING YOUR INSTRUMENT |
|---|---|
| Check again for the correct way to hold your instrument (see page 2). | Check again for the correct way to produce a tone on your instrument (see page 2). |

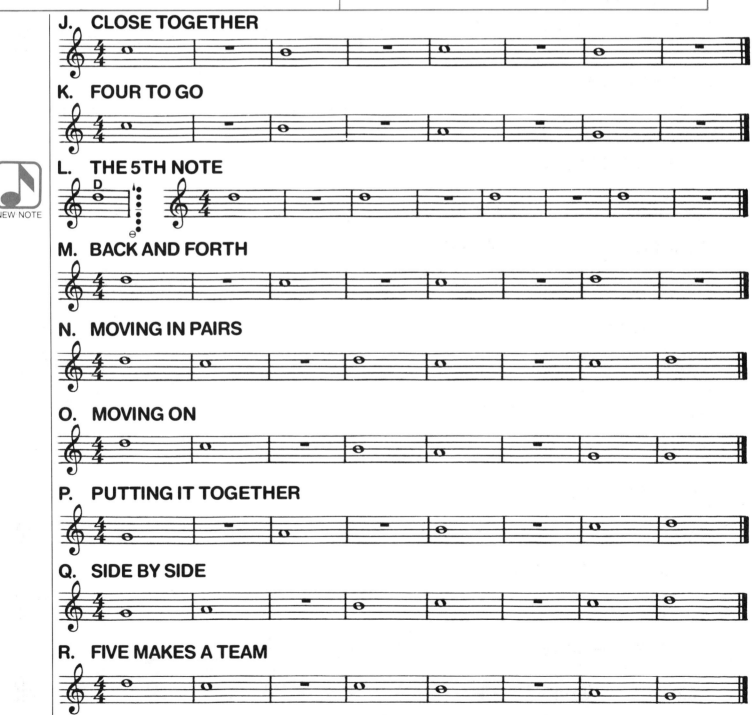

W3XE

# STARTING TOGETHER...

## THE BASICS

| KEYS | STAFF | TREBLE CLEF |
|------|-------|-------------|
| o = key open<br>● = key pressed down | <br>ledger line | <br>lines      spaces |

NEW NOTE

### 1. THE 1ST NOTE

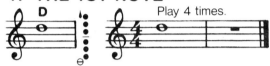

Play 4 times.

★ Remember the importance of air!

NEW NOTE

### 2. THE 2ND NOTE

Play 4 times.

### 3. WHAT A PAIR!

★ Write in the counting on the blank lines. (Your director will tell you the counting system to use.)

### 4. HOW DO YOU SOUND?

└ Band ┘ └ Brass ┘ └ Band ┘ └Woodwinds┘ └ Band ┘ └Percussion┘ └ Band ┘

★ Which section can play with the best tone quality?

NEW NOTE

### 5. THE 3RD NOTE

Play 4 times.

★ Don't "puff out" your cheeks!

### 6. TWO'S COMPANY

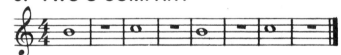

### 7. THREE TO GET READY

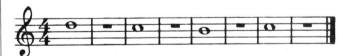

★ Are you playing with a good hand position and a full air stream?

### 8. A LITTLE EXTRA PRACTICE

THEORY GAME

### 9. NAME GAME

1. Write the names of the lines in the squares.

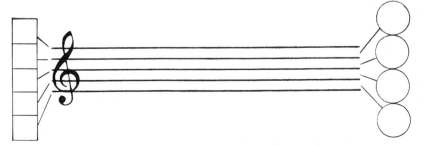

2. Write the names of the spaces in the circles.

# for the full band

| MEASURES | TIME SIGNATURE | WHOLE NOTE | WHOLE REST |
|---|---|---|---|
|  bar lines / measures | 4/4 = 4 beats in each measure | o = 4 beats | = 4 beats of silence |

**BREATH MARK** , Take a breath.

## 10. TWO AT A TIME
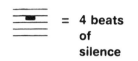

## 11. THE 4TH NOTE

A — Play 4 times.

## 12. THERE'S ALWAYS ROOM FOR MORE
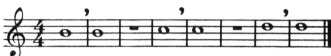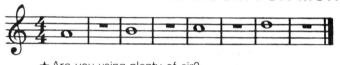
★ Are you using plenty of air?

## 13. THE 5TH NOTE

G — Play 4 times.

## 14. TWO-TIMERS
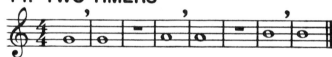

## 15. FIVE MAKES A TEAM

★ Write in the note names before you play.

| QUARTER NOTE | ♩ = 1 beat | |
|---|---|---|
| QUARTER REST | 𝄽 = 1 beat of silence | |

## 16. FOUR IN A ROW

★ Write in the counting before you play.

## 17. MOVING DOWN
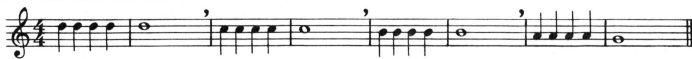

W3XE

NEW IDEA

| FERMATA<br>(sometimes called a "hold") | ⌢ | Play the note until your director signals you to stop. |
|---|---|---|

## 18. WARM-UP

A.    B. Play 2 times.

## 19. HOW DO YOU SOUND?

└ Band ─────────┘└ Woodwinds ┘└ Band ┘└ Brass ┘└ Band ─────────┘

★ Which section sounds the best?

## 20. IN CONCERT

A.                                                          Duet

★ Remember . . . rests are silent beats!

B.

NEW
IDEAS

| HALF NOTE | ♩ = 2 beats | 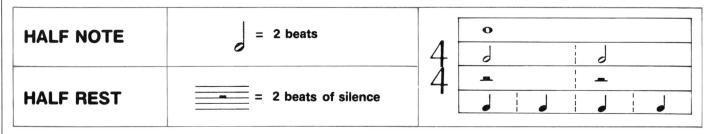 |
|---|---|---|
| HALF REST | ▬ = 2 beats of silence | |

## 21. HALF NOTE HAPPENING

★ Write in the counting before you play.

## 22. MAKING MUFFINS

English Traditional Song

★ Do you recognize this melody?

## 23. LITTLE ROBIN RED BREAST

Traditional

★ A full stream of air will make these melodies sound better.

## 24. MERRILY WE ROLL ALONG

Traditional

★ _ _ _ _ _ _ _ _ _ _ _ _ _ _ _ _ _ _ _ _ _ _ _ _ _ _ _ _
★ Write in the note names before you play.

## 25. WARM-UP

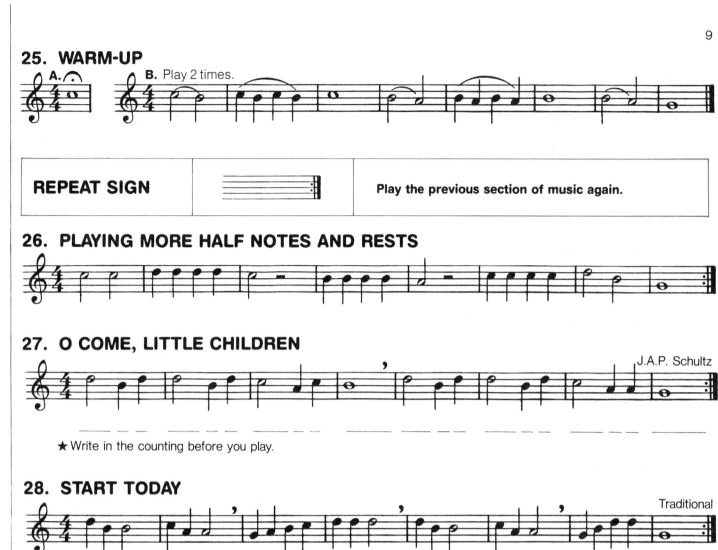

| REPEAT SIGN | | Play the previous section of music again. |

## 26. PLAYING MORE HALF NOTES AND RESTS

## 27. O COME, LITTLE CHILDREN

J.A.P. Schultz

★ Write in the counting before you play.

## 28. START TODAY

Traditional

## 29. FOLLOW THAT MAN

Root - Duet

## 30. FRENCH SONG

French Folk Song

## 31. SPELLING GAME

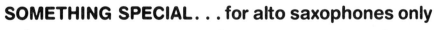

P R __ __ T I __ __ M __ K __ S P __ R __ __ __ __ T!

★ Write in the note names.

## SOMETHING SPECIAL... for alto saxophones only

★ Keep the air moving.

W3XE

## 32. WARM-UP

**A.**   **B.** Play 2 times.

NEW NOTE

## 33. READY FOR A NEW NOTE?

## 34. IN HARMONY

Duet

**A.**

**B.**

## 35. LIP AND TECHNIC BUILDER

★ Write in the counting before you play.

## 36. TOM DOOLEY AND HIS FRIEND

Folk Song - Duet

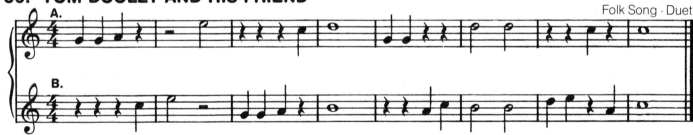

**A.**

**B.**

## 37. ODE TO JOY

Ludwig van Beethoven

★ Are you playing with a good hand position?

## SOMETHING SPECIAL . . . for alto saxophones only

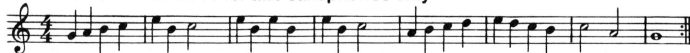

SPECIAL
EXERCISE

★ Are you getting a big tone?

W3XE

NEW IDEA

**EIGHTH NOTE**

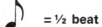 = ½ beat

An eighth note is half as long as a quarter note.

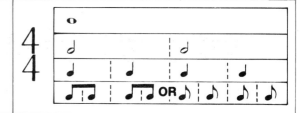

### 38. EIGHTH NOTE COUNTING AND PLAYING

1. Count the rhythm.  2. Write in the counting before you play.

### 39. CALYPSO SONG

### 40. CHA CHA RHYTHM

★ Write in the counting before you play.

### 41. YANKEE DOODLE CHA CHA

### 42. FEEL THE PULSE

★ Write in the counting before you play.

### 43. SQUARE DANCE

### 44. MOVIN' ON UP

★ Write in the counting before you play.

### 45. THE TALENT SHOW

### 46. UNEXPECTED EIGHTHS

W3XE

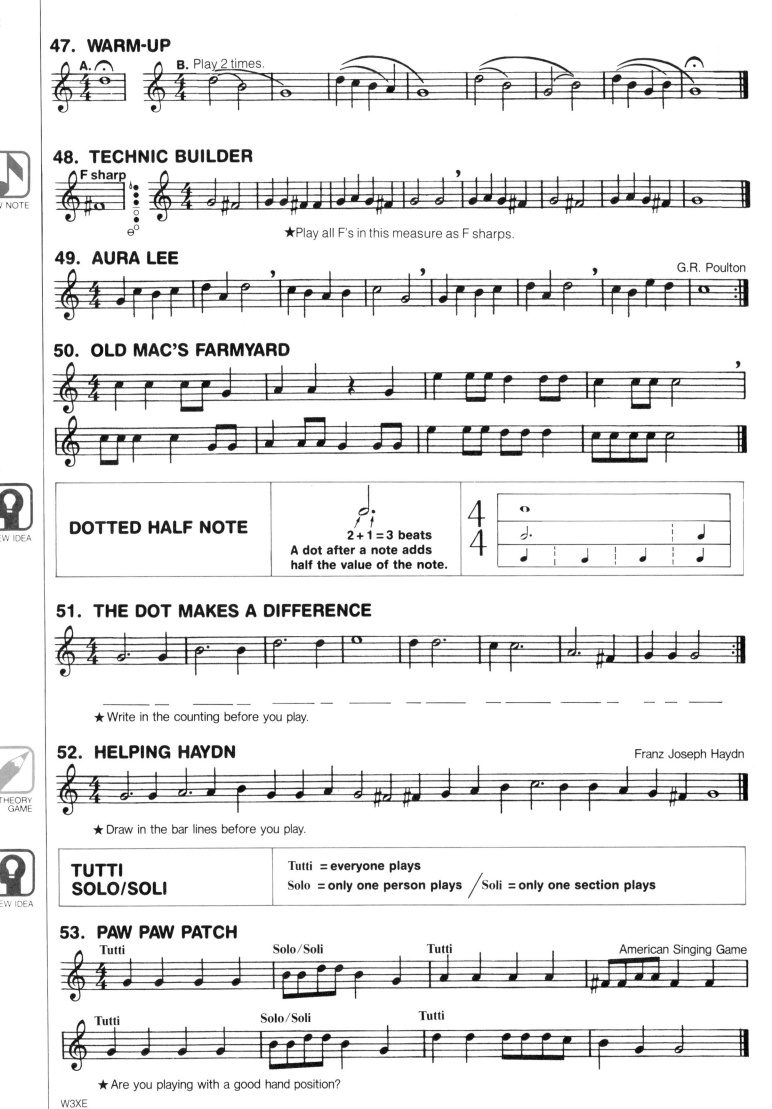

**47. WARM-UP**

**NEW NOTE**

**48. TECHNIC BUILDER**

★Play all F's in this measure as F sharps.

**49. AURA LEE**

G.R. Poulton

**50. OLD MAC'S FARMYARD**

**NEW IDEA**

| DOTTED HALF NOTE | 2 + 1 = 3 beats<br>A dot after a note adds<br>half the value of the note. | 4/4 |
|---|---|---|

**51. THE DOT MAKES A DIFFERENCE**

★Write in the counting before you play.

**THEORY GAME**

**52. HELPING HAYDN**

Franz Joseph Haydn

★Draw in the bar lines before you play.

**NEW IDEA**

| TUTTI<br>SOLO/SOLI | Tutti = everyone plays<br>Solo = only one person plays / Soli = only one section plays |
|---|---|

**53. PAW PAW PATCH**

Tutti        Solo/Soli        Tutti        American Singing Game

Tutti        Solo/Soli        Tutti

★Are you playing with a good hand position?

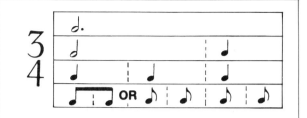

NEW IDEA

| TIME SIGNATURE | $\frac{3}{4}$ = 3 beats in each measure |  |

### 54. HEY, DIDDLE DIDDLE
Traditional

### 55. BLOW THE MAN DOWN
Traditional Sea Chantey

★ Write in the counting before you play.

NEW IDEA

| TIE |  | A tie is a curved line that connects two notes of the *same* pitch. Hold the note for the combined value of the two notes. |

### 56. THE TOTAL IS WHAT COUNTS

### 57. AUTUMN LEAVES ARE FALLING
German Folk Song - Duet

### 58. LOVELY EVENING
3-Part Round

### SOMETHING SPECIAL . . . for alto saxophones only

★ How's your wind speed?

### 59. RHYTHM PUZZLE

SPECIAL EXERCISE

THEORY GAME

1. Draw in the bar lines.   2. Clap the rhythm before you play.

W3XE

### 60. WARM-UP

| | | |
|---|---|---|
| **FLAT** | ♭ | A flat lowers a note 1/2 step. It remains in effect for the entire measure. You will first use a flat on page 15. |

### 61. TONE DEVELOPER

| | | |
|---|---|---|
| **KEY SIGNATURE** | | Key signatures change certain notes throughout a piece of music. When you see this key signature, play all the notes as naturals. |

### 62. LITTLE CABIN IN THE WOOD

Traditional

★ Did you check the key signature?

### 63. THE MAN ON THE FLYING TRAPEZE

George Leybourne

| | | |
|---|---|---|
| **SLUR** | | A slur is a curved line that connects two notes of *different* pitches. Tongue the first note and move to the second note without tonguing. Keep the air moving. |

### 64. SMOOTH SOUND

### 65. SLIPPERY SLURS

Tutti  Solo/Soli  Tutti  Solo/Soli

### 66. SPECIAL EFFECTS

★ Write a **T** under all the **ties** and an **S** under all the **slurs** before you play.

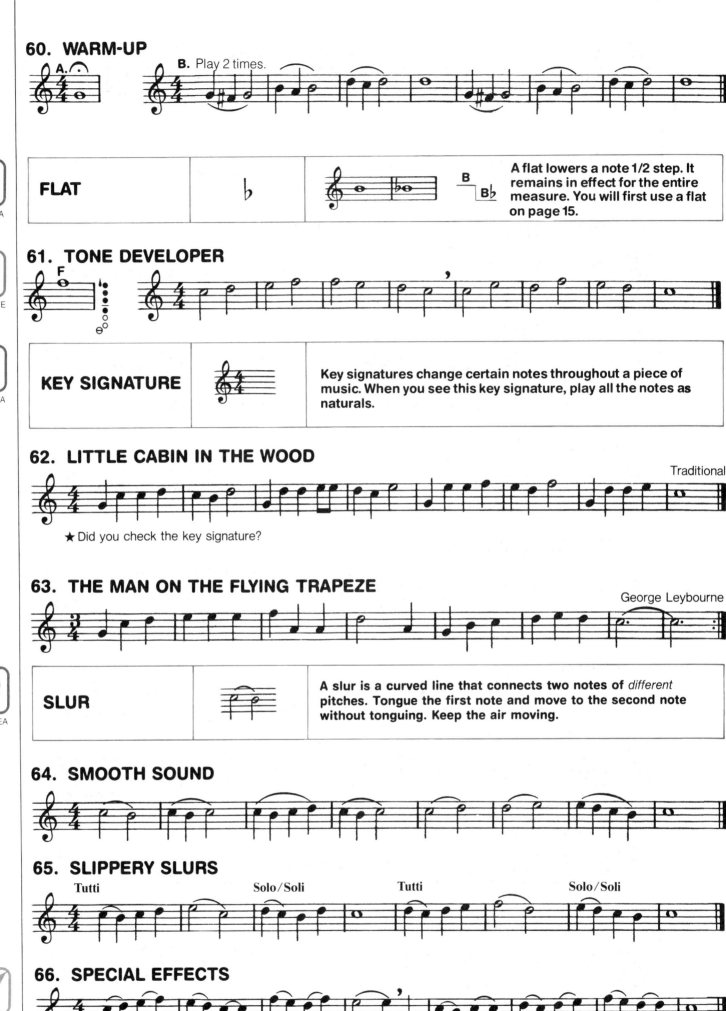

NEW IDEA

NEW NOTE

NEW IDEA

NEW IDEA

THEORY GAME

# SOMETHING SPECIAL . . . for alto saxophones only

| KEY SIGNATURE |  | When you see this key signature, play all F's as F sharps. |
|---|---|---|

## A. LONG TONES

## B. OCTAVE KEY FUN

★ Do NOT lift your thumb. Rock your thumb from the thumb rest to the octave key.

## C. NEW NOTES

NEW NOTE

F natural (♮)   Bb

## D. TECHNIC TRAINER

★ Did you check the key signature?

## E. FINGER FUN

★ Are you "rocking" your thumb to the octave key?

## F. THIRDS IN MOTION

## G. KNUCKLE BUSTER

## H. FINGER POWER

W3XE

16

## 67. WARM-UP

## 68. HOT CROSS BUNS

English Traditional Song

## 69. COPY CATS

★Is this an F sharp or an F natural?

**FIRST and SECOND ENDINGS**

**Play the first ending the first time. Then repeat the same music, skip the first ending, and play the second ending.**

## 70. POLLY WOLLY DOODLE

College Song

## 71. CAN YOU GUESS MY NAME?

## 72. BAND CHORDS

Band Arrangement

## 73. STREETS OF LAREDO

Folk Song - Band Arrangement

## 74. KEY SIGNATURE QUIZ

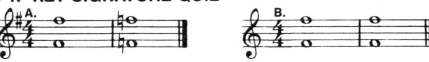

★Write in the note names.

W3XE

NEW IDEA

| NATURAL | ♮ | A natural sign cancels a flat or sharp. It remains in effect for the entire measure. |

## 75. WHO WILL PLAY ALL THE RIGHT NOTES?

## 76. WILL YOU GET TRICKED?

NEW IDEA

| TIME SIGNATURE | $\frac{2}{4}$ = 2 beats in each measure | 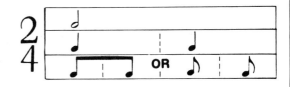 |

## 77. LITTLE BELLS OF WESTMINSTER

4-Part Round

★ Are you playing with a fast air stream and a good hand position?

## 78. THE HARPSICHORD PLAYER

Johann Sebastian Bach

★ Write in the counting before you play.

NEW IDEAS

| D.C. AL FINE | *D.C.* (Da Capo) = beginning<br>*Fine* = finish | When you see the *D. C. al Fine*, go back to the beginning and stop when you come to the *Fine*. |
| ABA FORM | | The first musical section A is followed by a new section B. Then section A is repeated. |

## 79. THE STAR GAZER

Folk Melody

*Fine*  *D. C. al Fine*

## 80. CONCERTO FOR HAND CLAPPERS, KNEE SLAPPERS, and FOOT STOMPERS

SPECIAL EXERCISE

NEW NOTE

## SOMETHING SPECIAL... for alto saxophones only

W3XE

18

### 81. WARM-UP

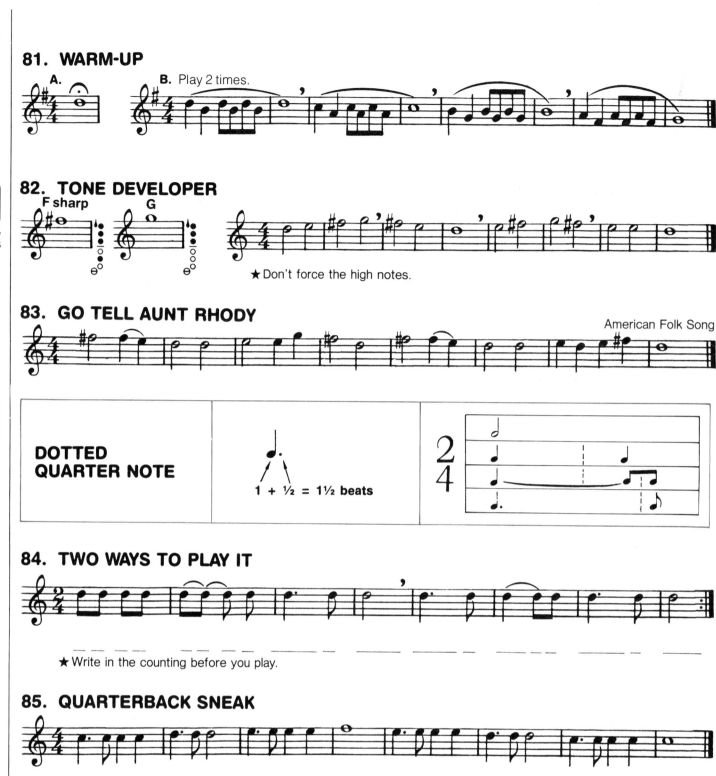

### 82. TONE DEVELOPER

**NEW NOTES**

F sharp    G

★Don't force the high notes.

### 83. GO TELL AUNT RHODY

American Folk Song

**NEW IDEA**

| DOTTED QUARTER NOTE | $1 + \frac{1}{2} = 1\frac{1}{2}$ beats | $\frac{2}{4}$ |
|---|---|---|

### 84. TWO WAYS TO PLAY IT

★Write in the counting before you play.

### 85. QUARTERBACK SNEAK

### 86. AMERICA

Henry Carey

★Are you using plenty of air?

### 87. FOLLOW THE LEADER

Solo/Soli    Tutti

*Fine*

Solo/Soli    Tutti

W3XE          *D. C. al Fine*

| **NEW IDEAS** | **DYNAMICS** | $f$ = *forte* <br> $p$ = *piano* | Play with a full volume. <br> Play with a soft volume. |
| | **PICK-UP NOTES** | | Note or notes that come before the first full measure of a piece. |

# WESTERN PORTRAIT

Root/Pearson

W3XE

SPECIAL
EXERCISES

# SOMETHING SPECIAL... for alto saxophones only

### A. WARM-UP SCALE

### B. THIRDS STUDY

### C. GOING UP?

★ Be sure you are NOT lifting your thumb. Rock your thumb from the thumb rest to the octave key.

### D. CHROMATIC FINGERING

NEW NOTE

★ Use the chromatic F sharp fingering.

### E. CHROMATIC FINGERING

NEW NOTE

★ Use the chromatic F sharp fingering.

### F. ARPEGGIO STUDY

### G. FINGER LIFTER

### H. SCALE WISE

### I. TECHNIC TRAINER

W3XE

NEW NOTE

## 88. WARM-UP SCALE

★ Is this an F natural or an F sharp?

## 89. RANGE FINDER

## 90. WILL YOU GET CAUGHT?

★ Be sure to use the chromatic F sharp fingerings.

## 91. FRERE JACQUES

4-Part Round

★ Are you tonguing properly? Remember to follow the tongue release with air.

## 92. FOREST GREEN

Folk Song

## 93. CLARINET CAPERS

## 94. MORE CLARINET CAPERS

## 95. MUFFINS RISING

English Traditional Song

## 96. HOOTCHY KOOTCHY

Traditional

## SOMETHING SPECIAL... for alto saxophones only

SPECIAL
EXERCISE

## 97. RHYTHM RAMBLE

THEORY
GAME

1. Draw in the bar lines.  2. Write in the counting before you play.

W3XE

## 98. WARM-UP

## 99. HOT CROSS BUNS

English Traditional Song

## 100. RAINY DAY

NEW NOTE

## 101. PRETZEL PARADE

## 102. MORNING HAS BROKEN

Gaelic Melody

## 103. MOLLY MALONE

Folk Song

★ Are you getting a nice big tone?

## 104. GOING TO THE RACES

Stephen Foster - Duet

## SOMETHING SPECIAL... for alto saxophones only

SPECIAL
EXERCISE

## 105. ACCIDENTAL GAME

THEORY
GAME

1. If the second note in each measure is lower than the first note, write **L** for **lower**.
2. If it is the same as the first, write **S** for **same**.
3. If it is higher than the first, write **H** for **higher**.

W3XE

## 106. SWEETLY SINGS THE DONKEY

2-Part Round

## 107. THE DONKEY SINGS IT IN A NEW KEY

2-Part Round

| TIME SIGNATURE | C = Common Time | C = 4/4 |
| --- | --- | --- |

**NEW IDEA**

## 108. LONG, LONG AGO

Thomas Haynes Bayly

★ Check the key signatures.

## 109. FIRST DOWN MARCH

Band Arrangement

| SHARP | ♯ | C C♯ | A sharp raises a note ½ step. It remains in effect for the entire measure. |
| --- | --- | --- | --- |

**NEW IDEA**

## 110. HERITAGE SONG

Henri Hemy

**NEW NOTE**

## 111. CHROMATIC MARCH

| ENHARMONIC TONES | SAME SAME | F F♯ G♭ F  G   Enharmonic tones are tones that sound the same but are written differently. |
| --- | --- | --- |

**NEW IDEA**

## 112. SAME GAME

G♭ _____  B♭ _____  G♯ _____  D♯ _____

★ Write the names of enharmonic tones that match the notes.

**THEORY GAME**

W3XE

### 113. WARM-UP

**A.**    **B.** Play 2 times.

NEW IDEA

| KEY SIGNATURE |  | When you see this key signature, play all F's as F sharps and all C's as C sharps. |

### 114. TECHNIC TRAINER

Fine    D.C. al Fine

★ Write in the counting before you play.

### 115. OUR DIRECTOR MARCH

F.E. Bigelow

### 116. KEY SIGNATURE CRAZE

**A.**    **B.**

### 117. AUSTRIAN MELODY

Franz Joseph Haydn

### 118. ENCORE PIECE FOR HAND CLAPPERS, KNEE SLAPPERS, and FOOT STOMPERS

Hand Clappers

Knee Slappers

Foot Stompers

### SOMETHING SPECIAL... for alto saxophones only

SPECIAL EXERCISE

W3XE

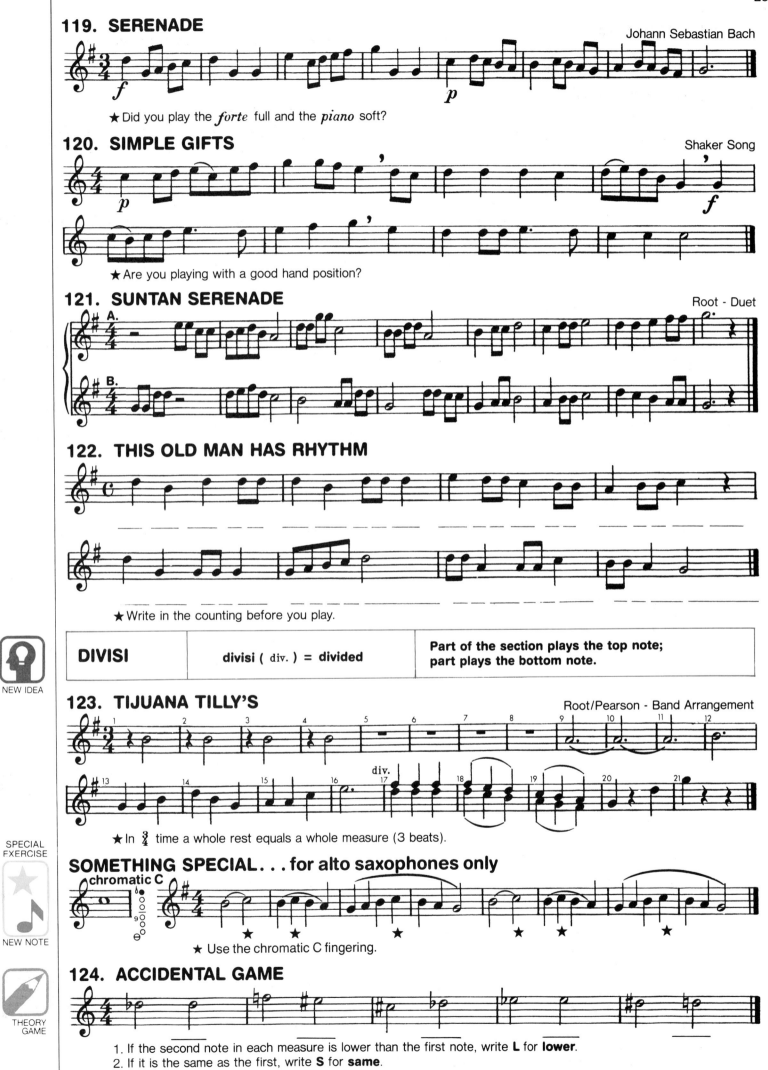

# SOMETHING SPECIAL... for alto saxophones only

### A. SCALE STUDY

### B. TECHNIC TRAINER

### C. GETTING THERE

### D. LET'S BOOGIE

★Be sure to use the chromatic F♯ fingerings.

### E. DO THE DIATONIC

### F. CHROMATIC CAPER

★Are you using the chromatic C fingering?

## 125. A CHROMATIC VIEW POINT

## 126. ACCIDENTAL ANTICS

★ Remember the key signature.

## 127. CROSSING THAT BREAK

★ Use plenty of air!

## 128. CHROMATIC MARCH RE-VISITED

NEW IDEA

| AABA FORM | The first musical section A is played two times, followed by a new section B. Then section A is repeated. |
|---|---|

## 129. ALL THROUGH THE NIGHT

Old Welsh Song - Band Arrangement

★ Listen for each section of the form.

## 130. SEE, THE CONQUERING HERO COMES

George Frideric Handel

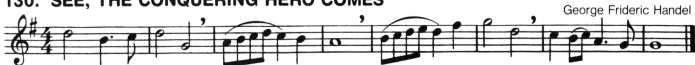

## 131. FOLLOW THE LEADER

THEORY GAME

## 132. NAME GAME

★ Write in the note names and their accidentals.

NEW IDEA

| DYNAMICS | <img_2 crescendo/decrescendo symbols> = crescendo (cresc.) <br> = decrescendo (decresc.) | **Gradually play louder.** <br> **Gradually play softer.** |

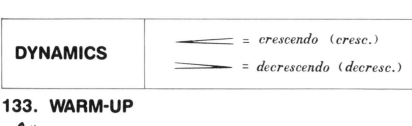

### 133. WARM-UP

### 134. BOOGIE BEAT

Root - Duet

### 135. CHROMATIC WALTZ

### 136. THE MINSTREL BOY

Folk Song

NEW IDEA

| THEME AND VARIATIONS | A simple tune followed by the same tune with changes. |

### 137. WHERE DID MY LITTLE DOG GO?

German Song

Theme

Variation

SPECIAL EXERCISE

### SOMETHING SPECIAL. . . for alto saxophones only

W3XE

NEW IDEA

| DYNAMICS | $mp$ = *mezzo piano* | Play with a medium soft volume. |
|---|---|---|
| | $mf$ = *mezzo forte* | Play with a medium full volume. |

### 138. SCARBOROUGH FAIR
English Folk Song

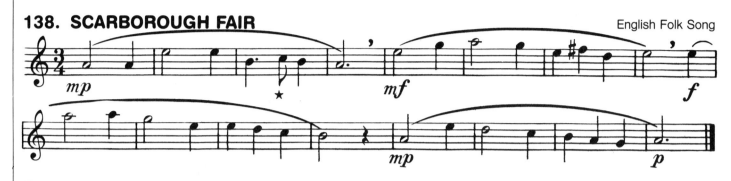

NEW IDEA

| PHRASE | A musical thought or sentence. The end of a phrase is a good place to take a breath. |
|---|---|

### 139. POLISHED PHRASES
Root - Band Arrangement

NEW IDEA

| TEMPOS | Andante = moderately slow<br>Moderato = moderate speed<br>Allegro = quick and lively |
|---|---|

### 140. BRING A TORCH
French Song

**Moderato**

★ Check your hand position.

### 141. BAYSIDE BOUNCE
Root/Pearson - Band Arrangement

**Allegro**

### 142. CHROMATIC CAPER

**Andante**

### 143. PUTTING IT ALL TOGETHER

★ Are you using a steady air stream?

## 144. HONEY ROCK FLAPJACKS

Band Arrangement

## 145. FROGGIE'S WALTZ

Root/Pearson - Trio

Spoken: "Rib-bit"

## 146. EARLY AMERICAN SALUTE

Billings/Pearson - Duet

## 147. JINGLE BELLS

Allegro

Pierpont/Pearson - Band Arrangement

## 148. COWBOYS AND CACTUS

Moderato

Root/Pearson - Band Arrangement

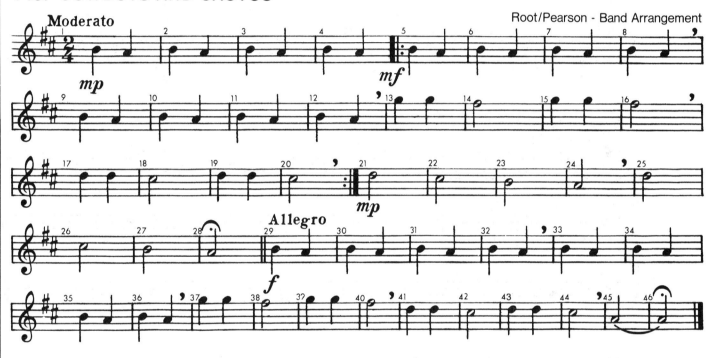

## 149. BUMPY ROAD

Band Arrangement

# IT'S ALL YOURS!

**This special page of solos is for extra practice and fun on your instrument.
The pieces may be played by themselves or along with the piano part found
in the piano accompaniment book.**

**JINGLE BELLS** — J.S. Pierpont

**GOOD KING WENCESLAS** — English Carol

**HOLIDAY GREETINGS** — English Carol

**GO, TEAM, GO!** — Go, Team, Go!

**SAINTS GO MARCHING IN** — Traditional

**AMERICA** — Henry Carey